Exploring Australia

Continents of the World
Geography Series

By
MICHAEL KRAMME, Ph.D.

COPYRIGHT © 2003 Mark Twain Media, Inc.

ISBN 1-58037-225-2

Printing No. CD-1571

Mark Twain Media, Inc., Publishers
Distributed by Carson-Dellosa Publishing Company, Inc.

Map Source: Mountain High Maps® Copyright © 1993 Digital Wisdom, Inc.

Table of Contents

The Continents

A continent is a large land-mass completely or mostly sur-rounded by water. Geographers list seven continents: North America, South America, Europe, Asia, Africa, Australia, and Antarctica. Greenland and the India-Pakistan area are sometimes referred to as "subconti-nents." Madagascar and the Seychelles Islands are often called "microcontinents." The island groups in the Pacific Ocean are called "Oceania," but they are not consid-ered a continent.

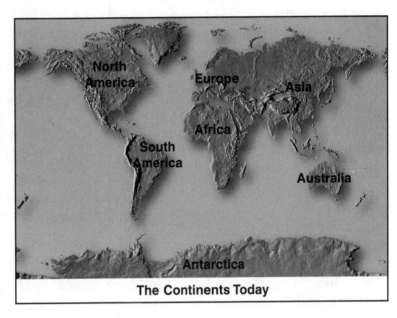

The Continents Today

The continents make up just over 29 percent of the earth's surface. They occupy about 57,100,000 square miles (148,000,000 sq. km). More than 65 percent of the land area is in the Northern Hemisphere.

HOW WERE THE CONTINENTS FORMED?

For many years, Europeans believed the continents were formed by a catastrophe or series of catastrophes, such as floods, earthquakes, and volcanoes. In 1596, a Dutch mapmaker, Abraham Ortelius, noted that the Americas' eastern coasts and the western coasts of Europe and Africa looked as if they fit together. He proposed that once they had been joined but later were torn apart.

Many years later, a German named Alfred Lothar Wegener published a book in which he explained his theory of the "**Continental Drift**." Wegener, like Ortelius, believed that the earth originally had one super continent. He named it **Pangaea** from the Greek word meaning "all lands." He believed that the large landmass was a lighter rock that floated on a heavier rock, like ice floats on water.

Wegener's theory stated that the land-masses were still moving at a rate of about one yard each century. Wegener believed that Pangaea existed in the Permian Age. Then Pangaea slowly divided into two con-tinents, the upper part, **Laurasia**, and the lower, **Gondwanaland**, during the Trias-sic Age.

Wegener's theoretical continent, Pangaea, during the Permian Age (white outlines indicate current conti-nents)

By the Jurassic Age, the land-masses had moved into what we could recognize as the seven continents, although they were still located near each other. Eventually, the continents "drifted" to their present locations.

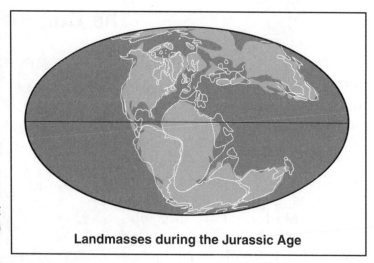

Landmasses during the Jurassic Age

Most scientists had been in agreement on the continental drift theory until researchers in the 1960s discovered several major mountain ranges on the ocean floor. These mountains suggested that the earth's crust consists of about 20 slabs or **plates**.

These discoveries led to a new theory, "**Plate Tectonics**," which has become more popular. This theory suggests that these plates move a few inches each year. In some places the plates are moving apart, while in others, the plates are colliding or scraping against each other.

Scientists also discovered that most volcanoes and earthquakes occur along the boundaries of the various plates. They hope that further study will help them increase their understanding of Earth's story.

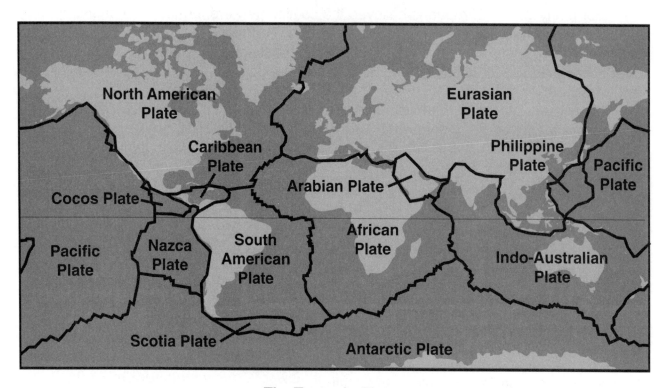

The Tectonic Plates

Name: _____ Date: _____

Questions for Consideration

1. What is a continent? _____

   _____

2. The continents make up what percentage of the earth's surface?

   _____

3. What was the name of Wegener's theory?

   _____

4. What is the name of the newer theory that replaced Wegener's?

   _____

5. What two natural happenings occur near the boundaries of the plates?

   _____

Map Project

On the map below, label all seven of the continents.

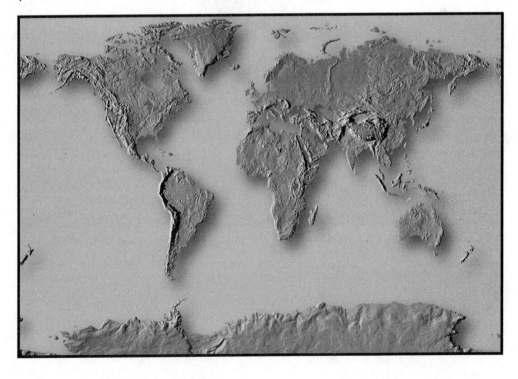

Name: _____ Date: _____

Outline Map of Australia

The Continent of Australia

The Australian outback is dry and rugged. Very few people live in the outback, or interior region, of the country.

Australia is the smallest continent in the world. It is also the world's only single-nation continent. Australia and Antarctica are the only continents located entirely south of the Equator.

Australia is about 2,500 miles (4,000 km) from east to west and 2,300 miles (3,700 km) from north to south. It covers 2,966,200 square miles (7,682,460 sq. km). It is about the same size as the continental United States.

Australia is southeast of Asia. The north coast of Australia is on the Arafura Sea, the Timor Sea, and the Torres Strait. The Coral Sea and the Tasman Sea are to the east of Australia, and the Indian Ocean is on the west coast. The southern coast is on the Indian Ocean and Bass Strait.

Australia has six states: New South Wales, Queensland, South Australia, Tasmania, Victoria, and Western Australia. It has two territories: the Australian Capital Territory and the Northern Territory. Australia and the island of Tasmania form the Commonwealth of Australia. The Commonwealth also governs the Territory of Ashmore, Cartier Islands, Australian Antarctic Territory, Christmas Island, Cocos Islands (also named the Keeling Islands), Coral Sea Islands Territory, the Territory of Heard Island, McDonald Islands, and Norfolk Island.

Australia is a flat continent. The interior region of the continent is called the **outback** and contains large plains.

The continent has four major geographic regions. The Great Dividing Range goes along the eastern coast. It includes a series of weathered mountains. One of these mountains, Mount Kosciusko, is Australia's highest point. It is only 7,310 feet (2,228 m) high.

Tasmania is an island off the south coast of the mainland. It is considered to be a separate region. Actually, it is a continuation of the Great Dividing Range, but it is divided from the rest of the continent by a strait.

The Central Lowlands is west of the Great Dividing Range. It contains grasslands and fertile river basins. The 1,600-mile-long (2,575 km) Murray River flows through this region.

The Western Plateau includes the western two-thirds of the continent. The soil is rocky and of little use for agriculture. However, many minerals are mined in the region.

Name: _____ Date: _____

Questions for Consideration

1. Where is Australia in relation to Asia?

    _____

2. How many states does Australia have?

    _____

3. What is Australia's highest mountain?

    _____

4. What major river flows through the Central Lowlands?

    _____

5. How much of Australia does the Western Plateau occupy?

    _____

Map Project

Using an atlas or globe and the outline map of Australia (located on page 4), label the following:

Bodies of Water:

Arafura Sea

Coral Sea

Great Australian Bight

Gulf of Carpentaria

Indian Ocean

Pacific Ocean

Tasman Sea

Timor Sea

Land Features:

Great Dividing Range

Great Sandy Desert

Great Victoria Desert

New South Wales

Northern Territory

Queensland

South Australia

Tasmania

Victoria

Western Australia

DID YOU KNOW?

Australia is the world's smallest continent and the sixth-largest country.

Australia's Climate

Australia has a variety of climates. Because it is an island, Australia's climates tend to be more moderate than the climates of other continents. The winds from the seas keep temperatures from reaching extremes.

Most of Australia is **desert**. The deserts and semiarid regions are in the central and western regions. About two-thirds of the continent receives less than ten inches of rain each year. Because of the continent's latitude, the sun evaporates most of this rain quickly.

Australia's northern regions experience a **tropical** climate. They have a hot, wet period during the monsoon season of February and March. A dry, warm period follows when the winds change from a northerly direction to southeasterly winds. In some of the tropical regions, annual rainfall exceeds 100 inches (2,540 mm).

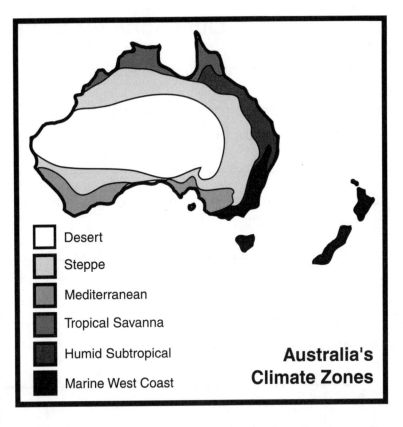

Legend:
- Desert
- Steppe
- Mediterranean
- Tropical Savanna
- Humid Subtropical
- Marine West Coast

Australia's Climate Zones

Further inland from the tropical region is the drier **savanna** area. Here, low rainfall is often supplemented by water from artesian wells. The grasses of this region support large herds of sheep and cattle. The herds are constantly moved, and grazing is carefully controlled to avoid depleting the grasses and the nutrients in the soil.

The southern regions of Australia have a **temperate** climate, with four distinct seasons. They have cool winters and warm summers. Often, the southern states receive hot, dry, summer winds from the continent's interior.

Part of the western coast has a **Mediterranean** climate. Here, there are hot, dry summers and mild, wet winters.

Tasmania and part of the southeast coast experience a **marine west coast** climate. A marine west coast climate has higher rainfall amounts and milder summers than a Mediterranean climate.

Snow is rare throughout the continent, except in the higher elevations of the mountains.

Each year, Australia experiences drought, floods, and cyclones. Brushfires are also common. In the Southern Hemisphere, cyclones have high winds that move in a clockwise direction. In the Northern Hemisphere, these winds move in a counterclockwise direction and are known as tornadoes.

Name: _____ Date: _____

Questions for Consideration

1. What keeps Australia's temperatures moderate?

   _____

2. When is Australia's monsoon season?

   _____

3. What are the two major sources of water in Australia's savanna regions?

   _____

4. What is Tasmania's climate type?

   _____

5. Where is snow common in Australia?

   _____

> **DID YOU KNOW?**
>
> Since Australia is in the Southern Hemisphere, its seasons are the reverse of those in the Northern Hemisphere. January and February are the warmest months, and June and July are the coldest.

Climate Zones

Describe the main features of the following climates:

1. Tropical: _____

   _____

2. Savanna: _____

   _____

3. Desert: _____

   _____

4. Temperate: _____

   _____

5. Mediterranean: _____

   _____

6. Marine west coast: _____

   _____

Australia's Resources and Industries

Agriculture was Australia's first major industry. Ranchers raised sheep for wool production and cattle for beef. Though a small percentage of land is available for farming, Australia is one of the world's major producers of beef and wheat and is the world's largest producer of wool. The invention of refrigeration techniques helped the nation become a major source of beef for Europe.

Because of poor soil, many Australian farmers use a rotation system of mixed crop and livestock farming. Often the land is used for grazing for several years, and then it is plowed for growing wheat. In recent years, the growing of grapes for wine has increased. Since most of Australia has a dry climate, farmers use irrigation to grow many of their crops. Today, major agricultural crops include wheat, barley, fruit, and sugar cane.

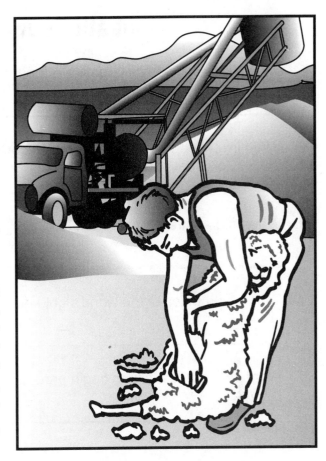

Opal mining and sheep ranching are two of Australia's major industries.

Australia is very rich in mineral resources. Deposits of important minerals are scattered throughout the continent. As miners discovered deposits of a variety of minerals, the mining industry became the continent's largest source of export income. The 1851 discovery of gold did much to increase Australia's population and improve its economy. In the 1850s, Australia produced over 40 percent of the world's gold. Today, Australia accounts for about one-eighth of the total annual world production of gold.

Other plentiful minerals on the continent include bauxite, coal, copper, diamonds, iron ore, lead, nickel, tin, tungsten, uranium, and zinc. In recent years, drillers have discovered vast oil and natural gas deposits in the center of the continent, as well as on the floor of the waters between the mainland and Tasmania.

Previously, Australia had provided raw materials to Britain but had done little manufacturing of its own. However, during World War I, Australia was cut off from Britain and had to produce many of its own manufactured goods. Since then, Australia's manufacturing industry has continued to grow. Today, Australia's factories produce machinery, equipment, textiles, chemicals, paper products, and wine. Many of these goods are produced for domestic use, but Australia has become one of the world's leading exporters. Japan purchases between 25 and 30 percent of all Australian exports each year.

Name: _____ Date: _____

Questions for Consideration

1. Australia is the world's largest producer of what agricultural product?

    _____

2. What invention helped Australia to become a major source of beef for Europe?

    _____

3. When did Australia's gold rush begin?

    _____

4. Today, how much of the world's gold does Australia produce?

    _____

5. What caused Australia to begin producing its own manufactured goods?

    _____

Matching

Match the items in the first column with the correct examples in the second column.

A. Agricultural

B. Mining

C. Manufacturing

_____ 1. Barley

_____ 2. Bauxite

_____ 3. Beef

_____ 4. Machinery

_____ 5. Paper

_____ 6. Textiles

_____ 7. Tungsten

_____ 8. Wheat

_____ 9. Wool

_____ 10. Zinc

DID YOU KNOW?

During the 1850s Australian gold rush, the population of the colony of Victoria increased 700 percent in just ten years.

Australia's Animal Life

There are many unique animals only found on the Australian continent. Clockwise from top right: Dingo, Kangaroo, Duck-billed Platypus, Wombat, and Koala

The most famous of Australia's native animals is the kangaroo. However, the kangaroo is only one of Australia's many unique animals. Not only does Australia have many animals not found anywhere else in the world, it does not have many animals common in the other continents. It is home to 240 species of mammals and 750 species of birds.

Unfortunately, many of Australia's unique animals have become extinct. Seven species of birds are extinct, and another 35 are endangered. Nineteen species of mammals are extinct, and another 63 are endangered.

The kangaroo is a member of the marsupial family. **Marsupials** carry their young in a pouch. The kangaroo can hop at speeds of up to 40 miles an hour (64 kph). Australia has about 50 species of kangaroo. Other Australian marsupials include bandicoots, koalas, wombats, and Tasmanian devils. Australia is also home to the world's only egg-laying mammals, the duck-billed platypus and the echidna, also known as the spiny anteater.

The dingo is a mammal believed to have evolved from the wolf and wild dog. Early natives used dingoes to hunt. Today, wild dingoes roam the countryside killing sheep and cattle.

Of the 750 species of birds, some of the more unusual include the albatross, penguin, bowerbird, budgerigar, cassowary, cockatoo, emu, gannet, kookaburra, lyrebird, and muttonbird.

Australian reptiles include two species of crocodiles and over 500 species of lizards, including the gecko, goanna, and skink. Over 100 species of poisonous snakes live in Australia; these include the copperhead, black snake, death adder, and tiger snake.

Since Australia is surrounded by water, its coastal waters have a variety of fish and water mammals. Several species of whales and sharks inhabit Australian waters. Fish and shellfish are also common. The Queensland lungfish is unique; it breathes through a lung rather than through gills.

Insects of the continent include many varieties of ants, bees, beetles, flies, and termites. The giant termites build hills that are up to 20 feet (6 m) high.

When the Europeans settled in Australia, they brought many species of animals to the continent. Many of these species became overpopulated and have endangered Australia's ecology and native species. Destructive non-native animals include foxes, horses, rabbits, and pigs.

Name: _____ Date: _____

Questions for Consideration

1. What is Australia's most famous animal?

   _____

2. How many species of Australian mammals are now extinct?

   _____

3. What family of animals carries its young in a pouch?

   _____

4. What Australian mammal is believed to descend from the wolf and wild dog?

   _____

5. What fish breathes through a lung rather than through gills?

   _____

> **DID YOU KNOW?**
>
> A baby kangaroo is only one inch long at birth. Some grow to a height of seven feet (2 m).

For Further Research

Choose one of the unusual animals mentioned in the narrative with which you are less familiar. Use at least two sources to help you. Write a paragraph in the space below describing this animal.

_____

_____

_____

_____

_____

_____

_____

_____

_____

_____

Australia's Plant Life

Australia has over 22,000 species of plants. Many of them are unique to the continent. Eighty-three species have become extinct since the 1700s, and another 840 are threatened with extinction.

Heavy forests cover much of the tropical regions. Ferns, cedars, oaks, palms, and a variety of vines are common here. Orchids often add splashes of color to the tropical forests.

Pine forests grow along the eastern coast and in Tasmania. Over 500 species of evergreens live in Australian forests.

The interior region, known as the **outback**, has little vegetation. However, some grasses and shrubs do grow in this region because they often have long root systems to enable them to absorb water in the outback's arid climate.

Many varieties of eucalyptus (left) grow in Australia. The golden wattle (right) is the national flower of Australia.

The eucalyptus is one of Australia's most important trees. It grows well in Australia because it is drought-tolerant and has few pests to harm its growth. More than 700 species of eucalyptus grow there. The karris and blue gums grow to over 300 feet tall. Other species, such as the dwarf shrub, grow to only one or two feet (less than one meter) in height.

Several varieties of eucalyptus are harvested for timber and material to make fiberboard and paper products. Oil distilled from the leaves is used to make medicine. Eucalyptus products are used as antiseptics and for healing; products include remedies for coughs and sore throats. Eucalyptus oil is also used as a scent for soap and other products.

The Aboriginal tribes used eucalyptus as a source of food, and often used the roots as a source of water. Eucalyptus leaves are a favorite food of koalas.

Several species of grass and shrubs cover much of Western Australia. Many of them are unique to the continent. Many of these grasses and shrubs provide food for the sheep and cattle herds.

A variety of native wildflowers grow throughout the land. Over 1,500 species of acacia exist; 1,000 of these are native to Australia. The golden wattle, a highly scented acacia, is the national flower of Australia. The Australians celebrate Wattle Day each September first. Gum from the acacia plant is harvested for making medicine. The Aborigines used acacia gum for toothaches, colds, and to heal wounds. They used acacia wood for clubs, shields, spears, and boomerangs.

Only six percent of Australia's land is suitable for growing crops. Wheat is the major crop grown for export. Barley and fruit are also major crops. Since Australia is a dry continent, some crops are grown in irrigated fields. Irrigated crops include citrus fruits, grapes, sugar cane, and rice.

Name: _____ Date: _____

Questions for Consideration

1. How many of Australia's plant species have become extinct?

   _____

2. What is Australia's most important tree?

   _____

3. What is Australia's national flower?

   _____

4. When is Wattle Day?

   _____

5. What is Australia's major export crop?

   _____

Matching

Match each use mentioned in the article that is listed in the first column with whether it is a product of the eucalyptus tree, the acacia plant, or both.

_____ 1. Antiseptics   A. Eucalyptus

_____ 2. Boomerangs

_____ 3. Fiberboard   B. Acacia

_____ 4. Food

_____ 5. Medicine   C. Both

_____ 6. Paper

_____ 7. Shields

_____ 8. Soap

_____ 9. Timber

_____ 10. Water source

DID YOU KNOW?

The state flower of Western Australia is the kangaroo paw. This flower looks like the paw of a kangaroo.

Australia's Islands

Many islands surround the Australian coast and are considered part of the continent. The largest and most populated of these is **Tasmania**, which is located off the southeastern coast of the mainland.

Tasmania was once connected to the mainland. Hobart is its capital. It also has many offshore islands, which include **Bruny**, the **Furneaux Islands**, the **Hunter Islands**, **King Island**, and **Macquarie Island**.

Australia also controls many other islands located farther off its coasts. Most of these islands are quite small and often uninhabited.

Australia's territory includes many islands.

Australia took possession of the **Norfolk Islands** in 1914. One-third of the Norfolk Islands is devoted to national parks and reserves. The islands have very fertile soil and a tropical rain forest climate. Bananas, citrus fruits, and coffee are major crops grown there. The islands achieved limited self-government in 1979.

The **Coral Sea Islands Territory** is quite small. It is administered from Norfolk Island. Only one of the islands, **Willis Island**, is inhabited. It has a population of four; these people are on the staff of a weather-reporting station.

The Territory of Ashmore and **Cartier Islands** are in the Indian Ocean. They came under Australian control in 1934. They are uninhabited, low islands made of coral and sand. They are administered as part of the Northern Territory.

The Territory of Heard Island and **McDonald Island** are tiny islands administered by the Department of Science. Britain transferred them to Australia in 1947. The islands are uninhabited and are a nature preserve for seals and a variety of bird species.

The Cocos Islands (also known as **the Keeling Islands**) are 27 small coral islands. They are 1,750 miles (2,816 km) northwest of Australia. The islands were discovered in 1609 but not inhabited until 1826. The residents voted to become part of Australia in 1984.

Christmas Island has an area of about 52 square miles (135 sq. km) and a population of 1,300. It is in the Indian Ocean, about 1,000 miles (1,609 km) from Australia. It is the top of a mountain, surrounded by a coral reef. Before it was explored, the captain of a ship that passed it on Christmas Day named it in honor of the holiday. It was annexed by Britain in 1888 and transferred to Australia by Britain in 1958. The Japanese occupied the island during World War II. It has phosphate deposits that are still being mined.

Australia claimed the **Australian Territory** of Antarctica in 1933. The territory covers over 2,362,000 square miles (6,117,580 sq. km) of sea and land.

Name: _____ Date: _____

Questions for Consideration

1. What is the largest island that is part of Australia?

   _____

2. How much of the Norfolk Islands is made up of national parks and preserves?

   _____

3. What is the population of Willis Island?

   _____

4. What is the population of Heard Island?

   _____

5. Who named Christmas Island?

   _____

Is Anybody Home?

Many of Australia's islands are uninhabited. In front of the name of each island or group of islands on the left, put a plus sign (+) if it is inhabited and a minus sign (-) if it is not.

_____ 1. Ashmore

_____ 2. Cartier

_____ 3. Christmas

_____ 4. Cocos (Keeling)

_____ 5. Heard

_____ 6. McDonald

_____ 7. Norfolk

_____ 8. Tasmania

_____ 9. Willis

DID YOU KNOW?

Many of Australia's islands are made of coral. Coral is made up of the skeletons of thousands of tiny sea organisms.

Answer Keys

THE CONTINENTS (page 3)
1. A large landmass completely or mostly surrounded by water
2. Just over 29%
3. Continental drift
4. Plate tectonics
5. Volcanoes and earthquakes

MAP PROJECT (page 3)
Teacher check map. Use the map on page 1 as a guide.

AUSTRALIA AT A GLANCE (page 6)
1. Over 2.9 million
2. Prime minister
3. Britain
4. Kangaroo and emu
5. January 26

MAP PROJECT (page 6)
Teacher check map. Use the map on page 5 as a guide.

THE CONTINENT OF AUSTRALIA (page 8)
1. Southeast of Asia
2. Six
3. Mount Kosciusko
4. The Murray River
5. Two-thirds

MAP PROJECT (page 8)
Teacher check map. Use the map on page 5 as a guide.

AUSTRALIA'S CLIMATE (page 10)
1. Winds from the seas
2. February and March
3. Rainfall and artesian wells
4. Marine west coast
5. The mountains

CLIMATE ZONES (page 10)
(Answers may vary.)
1. Tropical: hot temperatures; heavy rain
2. Savanna: low rainfall
3. Desert: dry
4. Temperate: cool winter, warm summers
5. Mediterranean: hot, dry summers; mild, wet winters
6. Marine west coast: higher rainfall and milder summers than Mediterranean climate

AUSTRALIA'S RESOURCES AND INDUSTRIES (page 12)
1. Wool
2. Refrigeration
3. 1851
4. One-eighth
5. It was cut off from Great Britain during World War I.

MATCHING (page 12)
1. A
2. B
3. A
4. C
5. C
6. C
7. B
8. A
9. A
10. B

AUSTRALIA'S ANIMAL LIFE (page 14)
1. Kangaroo
2. Nineteen
3. Marsupials
4. Dingo
5. Queensland lungfish

AUSTRALIA'S PLANT LIFE (page 16)
1. Eighty-three
2. Eucalyptus
3. The golden wattle
4. September 1
5. Wheat

MATCHING (page 16)
1. A
2. B
3. A
4. A
5. C
6. A
7. B
8. A
9. A
10. A

THE PEOPLE OF AUSTRALIA (page 18)
1. Seven people per square mile
2. Aboriginal tribes
3. The monarch of Great Britain
4. Eighty percent
5. About 24 percent

SEQUENCING (page 18)
1. 9
2. 5
3. 2
4. 7
5. 1
6. 8
7. 4
8. 6
9. 3

THE ABORIGINES (PAGE 20)
1. Over 500
2. To help them hunt
3. An object used as an emblem
4. About 60,000
5. Less than one percent

TRUE OR FALSE? (page 20)
1. -
2. -
3. +
4. -
5. -
6. +
7. +
8. -
9. -
10. -

AUSTRALIA'S HISTORY (page 22)
1. 1768 and in the 1770s
2. January 26
3. Convicts
4. 1901
5. 2000 Summer Olympics

SEQUENCING (page 22)
1. 8
2. 9
3. 6
4. 3
5. 1
6. 4
7. 2
8. 10
9. 5
10. 7

AUSTRALIA'S CITIES (page 24)
1. Almost two-thirds
2. Sydney
3. Melbourne
4. Sydney and Brisbane
5. Adelaide

NAME THAT CITY (page 24)
1. Melbourne, 3.3 million, Victoria
2. Brisbane, 1.4 million, Queensland
3. Canberra, 330,000, Australia
4. Sydney, 3.7 million, New South Wales
5. Adelaide, 1 million, South Australia
6. Perth, 1.2 million, Western Australia

AUSTRALIA'S ISLANDS (page 26)
1. Tasmania
2. One-third
3. Four
4. Zero
5. A ship's captain

IS ANYBODY HOME? (page 26)
1. -
2. -
3. +
4. +
5. -
6. -
7. +
8. +
9. +

Bibliography

Allison, Robert J. *Australia.* (Country Fact Files), Raintree/Steck Vaughn, 1996.

Boraas, Tracy, *Australia* (Countries and Cultures), Bridgestone Books, 2002.

Dahl, Michael S. *Australia.* (Countries of the World), Bridgestone Books, 1997.

Darlington, Robert. *Australia.* (Nations of the World), Raintree/Steck Vaughn, 2002.

Grupper, Jonathan. *Destination: Australia.* National Geographic Society, 2000.

Hintz, Martin and Ann Heinrichs. *Australia.* (Enchantment of the World), Children's Press, 1998.

Landau, Elaine. *Australia and New Zealand.* (True Books), Children's Press, 1999.

Landon, Lucinda. *Australia.* Econo-Clad Books, 1999.

McCollum, Sean. *Australia.* (Globe Trotters Club), Carolrhoda Books, 1999.

Moore, Jo Ellen. *Australia.* Evan-Moor Educational Publishers, 1999.

Parker, Lewis K. *Australia.* (Dropping In On), Rourke Book Co. Inc., 2002.

Peterson, David and James Taft. *Australia.* (True Books: Continents), Children's Press, 1998.

Wheatley, Nadia. *My Place.* Kane/Miller Book Pub., 1991.